MANY HEARTS, MANY LOVES, MANY POSSIBILITIES
The Polyamory Relationship Workbook

Christina Parker

MANY HEARTS, MANY LOVES, MANY POSSIBILITIES

The Polyamory Relationship Workbook

Christina Parker

Alfred Press
Hubbardston, Massachusetts

Alfred Press
12 Simond Hill Road
Hubbardston, MA 01452

Many Hearts, Many Loves, Many Possibilities:
The Polyamory Relationship Workbook
©2009 Christina Parker

ISBN 978-0-578-03503-1

Printed in cooperation with
Lulu Enterprises, Inc.
860 Aviation Parkway, Suite 300
Morrisville, NC 27560

This book is dedicated to my parents and everyone else who has ever claimed me as "family".

***

I would like to gratefully acknowledge the assistance of Raven Kaldera and Joshua Tenpenny. It is due to their efforts that this book is finally seeing the light of day.

I also want to offer my sincere gratitude for the advice and support I received from my partners (past and present) as I struggled through the process of compiling the material for this workbook.

Contents

Introduction

I have been thinking about writing a book on poly relationships for several years now. Unfortunately, I had two major obstacles to overcome before I could even begin. The first obstacle was that even though I have experienced very successful polyamorous relationships, the structure of those relationships is very unique, so I wasn't sure how valuable my experience would be for the majority of people investigating polyamory. The second obstacle was that while *my* relationship structures are very unique, there are very few common elements in the successful relationship structures I have encountered in observing other people's relationships. How could I possibly write a book with advice on how to have a successful polyamorous relationship when my experience has shown me that people who try to structure their relationships to fit what they think they are "supposed to be" are not very happy in those relationships?

I have been giving workshops on polyamorous relationships for many years, and I know that it is valuable for people to have me present my experience so that they can possibly learn from my mistakes and find some common elements that would work for them. However, the most valuable part of my workshops for many people is the Q&A period at the end where they are able to ask questions specific to their unique situations. I thought of writing a book in the format of providing answers to fictitious questions, but I was still worried that it would be too biased towards my own particular style and structure.

About this time, my first book, *The Path of Service – Guideposts for Excellence*, was published. (This book is an interactive journal/workbook for people who are pursuing a service lifestyle.) I was not sure how well this format would be received, since I was basically asking people to purchase a book that would be mostly written by the reader. However, the response so far has been even more positive than I would have imagined. In spite of that, I had not thought about using this format for a book on polyamorous relationships because, quite frankly, my ego kept telling me that I have a lot to say about polyamory that people need to hear. Also, it's a little weird being the "author" of a book that people write for themselves, and I wanted my second book to have more "meat" to it. However, when my (then) husband suggested that I use the workbook format for my book on polyamory, I instantly saw the wisdom of his suggestion.

Interestingly enough, shortly after I began to write this book, I entered into a new polyamorous relationship. Going through the process of negotiating that relationship and incorporating it into my existing relationships definitely contributed material for this book as my last experience with adding a new relationship was eight years previous. Unlike my other poly relationships, this new relationship did not have a Master/slave or D/s dynamic, so that gave me additional understanding of the challenges involved in a non-hierarchical relationship structure. OK, that's a lot of fancy words to describe what most people would see as a typical poly relationship, but the words "typical", "traditional", "boyfriend/girlfriend", etc. just don't adequately describe the new relationship. In reality, that is common with most poly relationships – they don't fit simple pre-existing labels because poly relationships involve a complexity of interaction that defies ordinary definitions. Anyway, not only was I happy to have the new relationship, I was pleased to have the additional experience to draw upon while writing this book.

Unfortunately, during the time I was writing this book, my relationship with my primary partner came to an end. We had been together over 10 years and this was the first time I had lost a poly relationship. The experience was painful but, as I did with the joyful experience of the new relationship, I have taken the lessons learned from the process and incorporated them into this book.

My goal for this book is to provide a tool for people who are exploring polyamory relationships, whether they are just taking their first steps on that journey or are experienced travelers. The exercises and information in this book are appropriate for anyone regardless of gender, sexual orientation, or life situation because it is your own personal "how to" book. It is designed to help you tell your own story and create your own roadmap. It is also designed to help you understand your partners' stories and read their roadmaps so you can determine where your paths will meet and where they will diverge.

My goal as the author of this book is to be your travel agent and occasional tour guide. I will help you prepare for the journey, point out places of interest to explore, and caution you about potential hazards. In the end, however, the decision about where to go and what to take with you is entirely your own.

How to Use this Book

This book is divided into sections representing areas or concepts to explore. Each section will contain an explanation of the concept and thoughts from the author. The first sections also include questions and hypothetical scenarios. The overall purpose of the exercises and material presented in the book is to foster self-exploration and improve communication skills.

Questions

The questions are designed to help build a clear picture of everything you bring to your relationships. Try to be as honest and thorough as possible with your answers because they will be providing the information you and your partners need to develop a successful relationship dynamic. Even if a question is not applicable to your situation, life is constantly changing and it may be applicable later. Even if you can't imagine the situation changing, it may be helpful to explain *why* you feel it does not apply to you. Also, I have included space in each section for you to write your own questions to answer that I did not think to include but you feel are important to consider.

Thoughts from the Author

The "thoughts" in this book are bits of advice and insight I have gathered during my own journey. I encourage you to use the space provided in this book to write a comment about each one. Do you agree with what I have written? Do you disagree with it? Does what I have written remind you of a specific incident you've experienced? Do you have additional comments to add to what I have written? The type of response you make is not important. What is important is that you think about what I have written and compose your own unique response.

Hypothetical Scenarios

The hypothetical scenarios in this book have been chosen to represent potential real-life situations that are commonly encountered in poly relationships. They are designed to help the reader anticipate reactions in similar situations and foster communication among partners. There are no right or wrong answers or solutions for the problems presented in the scenarios. The object is to look at the scenario from the viewpoint of each person in the scenario and decide how you would act, and how you would want your partners to act in a similar situation. While it may be more time-consuming than you would like to write full explanations of your opinions on each scenario, I encourage you to use the space provided to at least make some notes for yourself. This will help organize your thoughts on the scenario and make it easier for you to communicate those thoughts to your partner(s) later.

I strongly encourage you to give answers to the hypothetical scenarios that accurately reflect how you typically act and react to stress and conflict rather than answer with what you think you "should" do and feel in the situation. This book is a tool to help you understand yourself better so that you can use that understanding to make healthy, reasoned decisions. Among the many benefits I hope you will gain from using the hypothetical scenarios is a better understanding of your basic needs and communication styles that you might not have previously recognized.

General Advice

The blank lines in this book are more than just a way to fill pages. They are there for you to use. It doesn't matter whether you write lengthy essays, short paragraphs, a sentence, or just use single words as a way to make notes. Use the space in whatever works best for you, but use it. Not only will it solidify your thoughts and feelings on particular issues, but if you review the information in this book periodically it will provide a reference point for you to determine whether there have been changes in your life that might require alterations in your relationships.

While it will be invaluable for partners to share with each other the information recorded in this book, I strongly encourage each person to have their own copy and work through it individually rather than make it a collaborative effort. No, I am not just suggesting this because I want to sell more books. I am suggesting this because if you work through this with your partner(s) then it might be easy to fall into a trap of just saying what your partner(s) want to hear rather than what you really feel. In fact, for those of you who are already in relationships, it might be best to try and answer the questions as if you were single with no commitments to anyone but yourself. You do not need to wait until each person has completed the book to share and discuss answers, just keep the discussions to those sections that everyone has already had a chance to work through individually.

I will say, though, that you may want to think first about the nature of the poly relationship you want. I think this book will be valuable no matter what type of relationship you are seeking, but I also think that there are parts that will be unnecessary if you are only looking at a short-term relationship. The planning for a weekend trip to a city doesn't take much time because the consequences of overlooking something are small, but you want to make sure you are as prepared as possible if you are planning a three-month trek into the Amazon rain forests. As with everything else, I would suggest that you tailor your use of this book to what will work best for you and your partner.

A Few Disclaimers

The opinions expressed in this book are just that – opinions. The only "right" way to have a polyamorous relationship is the way that works for you and your partners.

Although I define it differently, for the purposes of this book I have used the word "partner" to refer to anyone in a relationship with another person. Since I am hopeful that this book will be useful in structuring any type of relationship, I wanted to use one term and let the reader interpret the meaning of that term in whatever way best fits the situation.

Since there are many different (and sometimes conflicting) definitions of terms related to polyamory, I think it is important for the reader to know that I define "polyamorous relationship" as any relationship that has a significant emotional, physical, mental, or spiritual connection. I do not think sexual interaction is necessarily a requirement for a relationship to be considered polyamorous in nature. I do, however, think there must be more of a connection than just one or two instances of sexual interaction for the relationship to be considered polyamorous. Finally, I also include "informed consent" from all partners in my definition of polyamorous relationship. This does not mean that all partners need to know or interact with each other, but they must know that the other relationships exist and have consented to be involved with someone who is non-monogamous.

Rather than continue to use the full words "polyamory" and "polyamorous", from here on I will be using the commonly accepted abbreviated term of "poly". If you are new to this lifestyle, it will help you get used to the terminology that you will find most often, and if you are not new to this lifestyle it will preserve the familiarity of language for you. (It also saves me a bit of typing, but I'm really doing this for you, honest!)

Bon Voyage!

-1-
Who Am I?

CONCEPT

Since this book is a tool to discover where you want your poly journey to take you, it is essential that you begin by examining who you are. Each journey requires different skills, knowledge, and tools. Later, when you decide what you want, it will be important for you to have a complete inventory of the assets you bring to a relationship so that you can determine if you have all of the necessary equipment. (OK, I was trying to avoid using words with double entendres, but the substitutes for "equipment" and "tools" sounded very awkward. It's difficult enough to try and write a book like this without worrying about hitting the thesaurus every five minutes to find a word that doesn't have an additional sexual meaning. So, let's make a deal. I'll try to minimize the double entendres if you will try to keep your giggles to a minimum when I can't avoid them.)

Although you may already have an idea of what you want in a relationship and how you'd like to structure it, it would be best to try and put those ideas aside while you are answering the following questions. The answers you give should reflect your present circumstances. The differences between what you possess and what you will need for your journey will be covered under the sections on negotiation and problem solving.

Also, if there is something that you possess but do not want to incorporate into your relationships, answer the question anyway. Whether or not you utilize something will be covered in later sections of this book. For example, if you live in a five-bedroom house but do not want a live-in partner, list the house because you still might have a use for it later that does not involve moving boxes and U-Haul trucks. Remember, this section is only about who you are and what you have, not what you want and what you will give.

QUESTIONS

> **Food for Thought**
> In my opinion, it is a moral obligation to disclose to your partners anything that has the potential to cause either of you harm. It is much better to suffer a few moments of embarrassment than a lifetime of guilt.

Comments:

Physical Characteristics:

- ❧ Age:
- ❧ Gender:
- ❧ Sexual Orientation:
- ❧ Health Concerns :
- ❧ Describe any piercings or tattoos you have:
- ❧ Birth Control Method:
- ❧ Safer Sex Methods (what you use and when you use it):
- ❧ Illegal Drug Use (be honest):
- ❧ Alcohol Use:
- ❧ Tobacco Use:

> **Food for Thought**
>
> One important consideration that is often overlooked when structuring poly relationships is basic logistics. While there may not be any limit to your capacity to love other people, there is a limit on the number of hours in a day. You may have room in your heart for more relationships, but is there room in your day?

Comments:

_____

_____

_____

_____

_____

_____

_____

_____

_____

_____

_____

_____

_____

_____

_____

_____

_____

_____

_____

Current Life Situation:

- ❧ Housing:
- ❧ Profession/Career Path:
- ❧ Work and/or Academic Schedule:
- ❧ Travel for Work (How often, how long, etc.):
- ❧ Income Level (Low, Average, High):
- ❧ Credit Rating (Excellent, Good, Fair, Bad):
- ❧ Education Level:
- ❧ Long Term Goals (business, school, family, moving to Antarctica, etc.):
- ❧ Are you able to relocate if necessary (why or why not)?:
- ❧ Children (If yes, list how many, and their ages):
- ❧ Custody Arrangements for Children (live-in or visitation schedule):
- ❧ Pets:
- ❧ Describe any other current life circumstances that would impact your relationships:

_____

_____

_____

_____

_____

_____

_____

_____

_____

_____

_____

_____

_____

_____

Food for Thought
Good relationships are like hot cocoa in front of the fire in a ski lodge. The warmth and sweetness are even better after enjoying the thrill of skiing down the mountain to get there.

Comments:

Fun and Relaxation:

- ❧ Hobbies:
- ❧ Sports (play and/or watch):
- ❧ Last book read:
- ❧ Favorite book:
- ❧ Favorite type of movie:
- ❧ Favorite weekend activity:
- ❧ Other significant sources of fun and relaxation in your life:

_____

_____

_____

_____

_____

_____

_____

_____

_____

_____

_____

_____

_____

_____

_____

_____

_____

_____

> **Food for Thought**
> Every partner you have has the ability to impact your other partners
> through you. To some extent, you are all in the relationship together so it is
> important that everyone knows who else is "in their bed".

Comments:

_____

_____

_____

_____

_____

_____

_____

_____

_____

_____

_____

_____

_____

_____

_____

_____

_____

_____

Relationship Status:

- Marital Status (legal and/or heart commitments):
- Other Poly Relationships (include information about the nature of each relationship such as level of commitment, type of interaction, or any other information would be necessary to understand the role that person plays in your life):
- List any partners who have "veto powers" or input on your potential poly partners:

Food for Thought
Words are symbols and the same symbol can mean different things to different people. For example, when I say "chair", I might actually be talking about a recliner but the other person might think "chair" means a wooden rocker. Effective communication can only happen when the people involved not only say the words but understand what the words mean to each person.

Comments:

_____

_____

_____

_____

_____

_____

_____

_____

_____

_____

_____

_____

_____

_____

_____

_____

_____

_____

_____

Personal Dictionary:

How do you define the following terms?
- Polyamory:
- Poly Relationship:
- Primary Relationship:
- Secondary Relationship:
- Casual Relationship:
- Committed Relationship:
- Poly Family:
- General Interaction (does it include phone, e-mail, IM, in person, etc.):
- Intimate interaction (does it include more than physical sex, etc.):

Food For Thought

Even with the best of intentions, we all have limitations on our abilities. Being honest with yourself and your partner(s) about your limitations will enable you to set realistic expectations for them. Although it does not directly pertain to poly relationships, I think the following is a good example of this concept in action. I enjoy seeing houseplants when I visit other people and I enjoy them in my own home. However, I don't buy houseplants for myself and I don't accept houseplants from people who expect to see them alive and well when they visit me because I am unable to keep them alive no matter how much I enjoy and appreciate them. I am not rejecting the gift of the houseplant; I am showing my respect for the value of that gift by not allowing it to be put in a position to be harmed.

Comments:

Basic Personality:

- In social settings, I am:
- My favorite environment to live in is (city, country, mountains, desert, etc.):
- My favorite environment to visit is:
- My greatest personality asset as a friend is:
- My greatest personality weakness as a friend is:
- My greatest personality asset in a poly relationship is:
- My greatest personality weakness in a poly relationship is:
- If I have a choice between going out or staying home, I generally choose:
- I normally express anger by:
- The emotion I feel most often is:
- When I have made a mistake, I usually:
- When conflict arises, I usually:
- Do you tend to either lead or follow in your relationships?:
- How competitive are you?:
- Describe the level of organization and tidiness you need to feel comfortable in your environment:
- Describe any additional personality traits that impact your relationships:

Food for Thought
One of the most important "trust relationships" you have is with yourself. Having trust in your own judgment will make it easier to trust other people.

Comments:

Core Values:

- ❧ I have the greatest respect for people who:
- ❧ I am most proud of my ability to:
- ❧ I find it unacceptable when my partner:
- ❧ I am more successful in my relationships or in my career (choose one and explain why):
- ❧ The three most important qualities in a partner are:
- ❧ How would you describe your political views?:
- ❧ Describe any other core values you possess that impact your relationships:

> **Food for Thought:**
> If you believe that people are made up of mind, body, and spirit then any time two people interact it is a spiritual experience.

Comments:

Spiritual Beliefs:

- My spiritual beliefs are:
- The most important things to me about my partner(s)' spiritual beliefs are:
- Describe how much of a role your spiritual beliefs play in your daily life:
- Describe any difficulties you have incorporating your spiritual practices into your daily life and poly lifestyle:

> ### Food for Thought
> Do not judge the success of your relationships by standards set by others. If all parties are happy and fulfilled then the relationship is a success even if you are "doing everything wrong" according to the "experts."

Comments:

_____

_____

_____

_____

_____

_____

_____

_____

_____

_____

_____

_____

_____

_____

_____

_____

_____

_____

_____

_____

Past Experiences:

- ❧ Describe your childhood family structure:
- ❧ How was conflict resolved in your biological family?
- ❧ Briefly describe your past poly relationships:
- ❧ Briefly describe how and why each relationship ended:
- ❧ Briefly describe your significant past monogamous relationships:
- ❧ Briefly describe how each relationship ended and why:
- ❧ What regrets (if any) do you have about the way past relationships have ended?
- ❧ What regrets (if any) do you have about the way you have behaved in your current relationships?
- ❧ Briefly discuss any experience you have interacting with other people who are living a poly lifestyle:
- ❧ Briefly describe your impression of the success of those relationships:
- ❧ Briefly describe any other past experiences that impact your relationships:

Food for Thought

Poly relationships can allow you to feel love and support on a level you never imagined was possible when they work. The key word there is "work". In order to feel that love and support, the relationships have to work for everyone involved – and everyone involved needs to work at the relationships.

Comments:

_____

_____

_____

_____

_____

_____

_____

_____

_____

_____

_____

_____

_____

_____

_____

_____

_____

_____

_____

Motivation:

- Why are you working through this book?
- What do you hope to gain from completing this book?
- Why do you think poly relationships will work for you?
- Describe how much (if anything) you are comfortable sharing about your poly relationships to people at work, family, and friends
- Do you think that you could be happy in a monogamous relationship?

_____

_____

_____

_____

_____

_____

_____

_____

_____

_____

_____

_____

_____

_____

_____

_____

_____

_____

Additional Questions:

_____

_____

_____

_____

_____

_____

_____

_____

_____

_____

_____

_____

_____

_____

_____

_____

_____

_____

_____

_____

_____

_____

_____

HYPOTHETICAL SCENARIOS

1. You and your current poly partner(s) have all completed the questions in this section. One partner is unwilling to share his/her answers to all or some of the questions.

    Briefly describe how you would feel and how you would handle it if you were the partner who did not want to share answers.

    Briefly describe how you would feel and how you would handle the situation if you were the partner who was denied access to the answers.

2. Imagine the same scenario with a prospective partner who does not wish to share answers.

Briefly describe how you would feel and how you would handle it if you were the prospective partner who did not want to share answers.

Briefly describe how you would feel and how you would handle it if you were the prospective partner who was denied access to the answers.

❧ Additional information you believe is important for others to know about you:

_____

_____

_____

_____

_____

_____

_____

_____

_____

_____

_____

_____

_____

_____

_____

_____

_____

_____

_____

_____

_____

_____

-2-
What Do I Want in a Poly Relationship?

CONCEPT:

Have you ever heard a 3-year-old in a toy store? Most likely, what you have heard is the same every time – "I want, I want, I want!" This is the part of the book where you get to be that 3-year-old. In the first section, you were asked to answer the questions without taking into consideration what you want. In this section, it will be most effective if you forget what you have and focus solely on what you want.

You may find that you want things that are completely in opposition to each other. You may also find that what you want is incompatible with who you are and what you have. Oddly enough, you will probably find that you want things that are also incompatible with what you need. Do not let those inconsistencies stop you. You are the 3-year-old, remember? The 3-year-old isn't going to let logic and reason stand in the way of expressing wants and, for this section at least, neither should you. The contradictions and inconsistencies will get sorted out in the sections that follow.

Another trait of 3-year-olds that will be helpful here is inconsistency. Sometimes the 3-year-old must have the teddy bear and sometimes the 3-year-old does not want the teddy bear. This could also be true for you in your poly relationships. You may find that you want something with one partner but not with another.

I have one last little push to get you going. A 3-year-old doesn't worry about being greedy or selfish. Let your imagination and fantasies run free. Don't worry about anyone or anything else except you. For now, just walk up and down every aisle in the store, look at everything on every shelf, and if something looks good, point and say "I want!" If all else fails, imagine that your parents are about to take you (the 3-year-old) on a cross-country car trip, and they want you to have anything and everything that will keep you from being bored and cranky on that trip.

QUESTIONS

> **Food for Thought**
> While it can be a recipe for disaster to base a relationship solely on physical attraction, I think it is very important to find your partner physically attractive if the relationship will involve sexual interaction. You are not doing your prospective partner any favors by pursuing the relationship without that attraction. Everyone deserves to have a partner who finds them attractive. Beauty is in the eye of the beholder and just because you do not find the person attractive, please remember that there will be many other people out there who do.

Comments:

_____

_____

_____

_____

_____

_____

_____

_____

_____

_____

_____

_____

_____

_____

_____

_____

_____

Physical Considerations:

- ❧ Describe the physical characteristics you want in a partner:
- ❧ Do you want a sexual relationship with a partner?
- ❧ What sexual orientation do you want in a partner?
- ❧ How do you want a partner to feel about illegal drug use?
- ❧ How do you want a partner to feel about alcohol use?
- ❧ How do you want a partner to feel about tobacco use?
- ❧ Describe any tattoos or piercings you might want a partner to have:
- ❧ Describe any particular sexual fetishes or kinks that you want to share with a partner:

> ## Food for Thought
> Structures are much easier to change than emotions. One of the reasons it is so important to have a unique structure for each relationship is that oftentimes what we want emotionally from one partner could be uncomfortable if it comes from a different partner. For example, you may feel uplifted by a strong bond of romance with one partner but feel burdened by too much romance from another partner.

Comments:

_____

_____

_____

_____

_____

_____

_____

_____

_____

_____

_____

_____

_____

_____

_____

_____

_____

_____

Emotional Considerations:

- Describe the level of relationship focus you want with your partners (for example, do you want them somewhere in your thoughts at all times or do you want to be able to let your focus shift completely away from the relationship at times?):
- Do you want a romantic connection with a partner?
- Do you want a casual relationship with little or no commitment?
- Describe the level and type of commitment you want with a partner:
- What frequency of contact do you want with a partner (daily, weekly, etc.):
- Do you want a partner who currently has other relationships?
- What types of other relationships do you want a partner to have?
- Do you want a partner who will not have any other relationships?
- How much do you want your family to know about your partner and your relationship?
- How much do you want your friends to know about your partner and your relationship?
- If a partner has children, describe the relationship you would like to have with them:
- What qualities do you want in a partner to help counteract what you see as your weaknesses?
- What personality traits do you want in a partner?
- Do you want to keep parts of your relationship(s) private from your other partners? If so, what?

Food for Thought
One of the most intimate connections two people can share is a strong spiritual bond. When considering what you want in a spiritual connection, it is important to examine how much intimacy you want in the relationship overall and let that guide your wants for spiritual connection with a partner.

Comments:

Spiritual Considerations:

- Describe the level of spiritual connection you want in a partner:
- Do you want a partner who shares your spiritual beliefs?
- If your spiritual beliefs include religious practices, do you want a partner who will participate in those practices with you?

> **Food for Thought**
> One big stumbling block to getting what you want in a poly relationship can be simple logistics. The laws of physics, space and time are impossible to ignore. However, with a little creativity and pre-planning, you can often get a lot more of what you want than you initially thought would be possible.

Comments:

Logistical Considerations:

- ❧ Do you want a partner that you consider to be living "local" to you?
- ❧ Do you want a partner that you consider to be a long distance relationship?
- ❧ Describe what housing situation you would like a partner to have:
- ❧ Do you want a partner with pets?
- ❧ Do you want a partner who is organized and tidy?
- ❧ Do you want a partner who is relaxed about time frames and physical clutter?
- ❧ Describe what type of scheduled interaction you want with a partner:
- ❧ Do you want spontaneous interaction with a partner if it is mutually convenient?
- ❧ Do you want to keep joint finances with a partner?
- ❧ Describe the financial status and credit situation you want a partner to have:
- ❧ Do you want to have children with a partner?
- ❧ Describe what you want in regard to a partner who is already a parent:
- ❧ Do you want a partner with a similar lifestyle to yours?

Food for Thought
Never underestimate the value of a good conversation.

Comments:

Mental Considerations:

- ஒ Describe which (if any) of your interests you want a partner to share:
- ஒ List any special interests/talents you would like in a partner that you do not have but would like to learn (for example, ballroom dancing, kayaking, astronomy):
- ஒ Do you want a partner with an active social life?
- ஒ Do you want a partner who mostly enjoys spending quiet time at home?
- ஒ Do you want someone who is not sure what lies ahead in his/her life?
- ஒ Do you want a partner who has his/her life planned and goals set?
- ஒ Do you want a partner who will help you achieve or set your goals?
- ஒ What political views do you want a partner to have in common with you?

> ### Food for Thought
> Every person is different, and each of your poly relationships will be different because they will be with different people. If you find yourself making unfavorable comparisons among your relationships, remember to compare the relationship structures as well. You will naturally have more conflict with the person that shares the household chores with you than the person you only see in a hotel where there are no chores or distractions to interfere with relaxation and play time. I don't believe there is anything wrong with structuring a poly relationship in a way that does not incorporate the realities of daily living as long as everyone acknowledges the differences.

Comments:

Structural Considerations:

- ❧ What structure do you want for your poly relationships?
- ❧ Do you want to create that structure from scratch or join an existing structure?
- ❧

Other Considerations

• Describe any other wants you have for your poly relationships that have not been listed in this section:

_____

_____

_____

_____

_____

_____

_____

_____

_____

_____

_____

_____

_____

_____

_____

_____

_____

_____

_____

_____

_____

Additional Questions:

HYPOTHETICAL SCENARIOS

1. Your partner reads your list of wants and gets upset because he/she feels that he/she can't fulfill most of them. How do you feel and what do you do?

2. Imagine the same scenario, only this time you are the partner who feels you can't fulfill most of the wants on your partner's list. How do you feel about yourself? How do you feel about your partner? What do you do?

3. Several months after filling out this section of the book, your partner comes to you and says that most of the wants he/she listed are not exactly accurate because they were based on what your partner thought you wanted rather than what your partner really wanted. What do you do and how do you feel?

4. Imagine the same scenario, only this time you are the one who has realized that the wants you wrote were more based on how you thought your partner would want you to answer. How do you feel and what do you do?

5. Your partner starts a new relationship and after a few months you begin to feel that the new person's actions do not really reflect what he/she said that he/she wants in the relationship. How you do you feel and what do you do?

6. Imagine the same scenario, only this time you are the partner who has the new relationship that is causing concern for your existing partner. How do you feel and what do you do?

7. Imagine the same scenario, only this time you are the new partner that is causing the doubts in the existing partner. How do you feel and what do you do?

-3-
What Do I Need in a Poly Relationship?

CONCEPT

As much fun as it can be acting like a 3-year-old in a toy store, we all know now that there is a price to pay for everything. Some things are worth paying the price to have, some things cost more than they are worth, and some things we simply can't afford to have because the price is too high. Usually, what determines whether we get what we want is dependent on our resources and needs. After we have used our resources to meet our needs, whatever is left over can be used to get what we want.

Needs are very tricky things. Everyone has them, but not everyone has the same ones. For example, we all need to eat and sleep, but bodybuilders have much different needs for food and rest than the average person requires to maintain their current state of health. It is easy and obvious to see that human beings have physical needs and to recognize the signs that those needs are not being met. It is not so obvious to see that human beings also have emotional, mental, and spiritual needs as well. Those needs are just as important to acknowledge and respect as physical needs. Unfortunately, it is harder to recognize the signs that those needs are not being met – even if it is your own needs that require attention. Lifestyle changes can reduce or increase our needs, but those changes are not easily made. It is much easier to be able to recognize what we need and communicate those needs to our partner(s) so that those needs can be met.

Sometimes it is hard to distinguish between wants and needs. One way to make that distinction is that needs are things that will diminish you if they are not met. Wants, however, are things that can add pleasure to life and sometimes can help speed the healing process when needs have been neglected, but wants are also things that may diminish you if you get too much of them. Needs are things that keep us healthy and balanced. Wants are things that need to be managed so that we can stay healthy and balanced.

Determining your needs and structuring your relationships to meet those needs is the key to successful relationships – poly or otherwise. Most of our basic needs we can meet on our own. This section focuses on needs that are directly related to your relationships. Also, you may not need the same things in all of your relationships so make sure to specify the differences when answering the questions.

QUESTIONS

> ### Food for Thought
> It is impossible to be honest with someone else if you are not honest with yourself first.

Comments:

_____

_____

_____

_____

_____

_____

_____

_____

_____

_____

_____

_____

_____

_____

_____

_____

_____

_____

_____

_____

_____

Physical Considerations:

- Describe the physical characteristics you need in a partner:
- Do you need to have a sexual relationship with a partner?
- If so, describe what you need in a sexual relationship with a partner:
- Describe your needs from a partner regarding affection:
- Describe your needs from a partner regarding tobacco, alcohol, and illegal drug use:
- Describe any specific diet style needs you have from a partner:
- Describe any needs you have from a partner regarding general lifestyle:

> **Food for Thought**
> I have found that the biggest obstacle I face is my own insecurity. When I am feeling insecure, my actions are tentative and my feelings are easily hurt. When I am feeling confident, my actions are purposeful and I do not let little things diminish my happiness.

Comments:

Emotional Considerations:

- ❧ Describe the type and level of relationship focus you need with your partners (as in the previous chapter, do you need them to be somewhere in your thoughts at all times or do you want to be able to let your focus shift completely away from the relationship at times?):
- ❧ Describe the level and type of commitment you need from a partner:
- ❧ What minimum frequency of contact do you need with a partner (daily, weekly, etc.):
- ❧ How much acknowledgement of your relationship with your partner do you need from friends, family, children, etc.?
- ❧ Do you need to keep parts of your relationship(s) private from your other partners? If so, what?
- ❧ What personality traits do you need in a partner?

_____

_____

_____

_____

_____

_____

_____

_____

_____

_____

_____

_____

_____

_____

_____

_____

_____

_____

> ### Food for Thought
>
> When I first began examining my needs in my relationships, I focused solely on my physical and emotional needs. When I began to see myself as a combination of mind, body and spirit, I also began to see that my third aspect of spirit had needs that were just as important to consider as the needs of my mind and body. Those needs are difficult to understand, and even more difficult to identify when they are not being met. I have found, however, that sometimes what feels like a deficiency in my physical or emotional needs is really a symptom of my spiritual needs being neglected.

Comments:

Spiritual Considerations:

- Describe the needs you have from a partner regarding your personal spiritual beliefs:
- Describe any other spiritual needs you require from a partner:

Food for Thought

While it is easy to see and understand that all living things have different physical needs that cause them to thrive or wither in different physical environments, it is sometimes harder to understand that this applies to human beings as well. Our technology allows us to physically survive in even the harshest conditions. However, our mind, body, and spirit are all connected. Even though humans have adapted to physically survive in any environment, those adaptations are not always able to compensate for the emotional and spiritual effects of an unhealthy environment. We need to remember that we all have different spiritual and emotional needs so it makes sense that one person will thrive in an environment that will cause another person to wither.

Comments:

_____

_____

_____

_____

_____

_____

_____

_____

_____

_____

_____

_____

_____

_____

_____

_____

Logistical Considerations:

- Describe any needs you have from a partner regarding living arrangements and locations:
- Describe any needs you have from a partner regarding financial matters:

Food for Thought

One of the things that keeps me growing as a person is the stimulation I receive from my mental connections and interests shared with my partners.

Comments:

Mental Considerations:

❧ Describe what level of knowledge of and/or desire to share your interests you need from a partner:

❧ Do you need a partner that has the same or different thinking/reasoning style as you?

❧ Describe your needs from a partner regarding political views:

Food for Thought
In my opinion, ethics and core values are not black and white. I find it perfectly acceptable that what is "right" for one person may be completely "wrong" for another. At a bare minimum, compatibility in ethics is essential for a healthy relationship. I do not need to have my partners agree with my personal values, but I do need for them to accept me even when they disagree with me.

Comments:

Core Values:

- Describe what core values you need a partner to share with you:
- Describe what core values you need a partner to accept but do not need to be shared:

Other Considerations:

&❧ Describe any other needs you have from your poly relationships that have not been listed in this section:

_____

_____

_____

_____

_____

_____

_____

_____

_____

_____

_____

_____

_____

_____

_____

_____

_____

_____

_____

_____

HYPOTHETICAL SCENARIOS

1. There are no hypothetical scenarios for this section because all of the hypothetical scenarios in this book are designed to help you identify and understand your needs. Instead, after you have completed the rest of this book, review your answers to the hypothetical scenarios. Describe any new or additional thoughts you have regarding your needs after reading through your answers to the questions in the hypothetical scenarios.

-4-
What Are My Fears about Poly Relationships?

CONCEPT:

Exploring poly relationships can be exciting and fun, but it can be scary and painful at the same time. With any new relationship comes change, risk, and uncertainty. When you already have established relationships, the stakes are even higher because the new relationship has the potential to damage the existing relationships. The more you have, the more you stand to lose if something goes wrong so it is wise to be cautious. There is a danger, however, in letting that reasonable, healthy caution become unreasonable, unhealthy worry and fear. While it is doubtful that you will ever completely overcome all of your fears, understanding your fears and why you have them can be the key to minimizing the negative impact those fears have on you and your relationships.

Virtually every worry or fear that people experience in poly relationships stems from one of two sources – jealousy and envy. Although many people use those terms interchangeably, the causes of those emotions are very different and knowing those differences is critical to resolving and eliminating the problems that result from those emotions. In fact, I consider the following analysis of jealousy and envy to be the most valuable information in this book.

Jealousy is caused by the fear of losing your relationship. Even if you feel completely secure that the relationship will last, you can still experience jealousy from a fear of losing a part of the relationship you value. When you experience jealousy, it should be a big red flag to you that there is something in your relationship that is causing you to feel insecure. It may not be easy, but once that insecurity has been eliminated, the jealousy will disappear with it.

Envy, on the other hand, is not really caused by fear but by a perceived deficiency in your relationship. Envy stems from wanting or needing what someone else has. Sometimes the envy can come from wanting to have something "exclusively" with your partner, and sometimes it is a matter of just wanting to share the same things with your partner that he or she is sharing with someone else. Many times the resolution is found by simply communicating to your partner that you have this want or need. There may be times when your partner will be unable to meet this want or need (for example, it may violate a previously existing agreement with another partner). Even if your partner is unable or unwilling to meet the need or want that caused your envy, discussing the situation with your partner can often enable you to gain the insight and understanding necessary to still let go of your envy.

QUESTIONS

Food for Thought
You are uniquely you. Just as none of your partners can completely
replace another, no one can ever completely replace you.

Comments:

- What fears or concerns do you have regarding your ability to meet your poly partners' needs and wants?
- What concerns do you have regarding the impact of a new relationship on your existing relationships?
- Describe the insecurities you currently experience in your relationships:
- What types of behavior in your partner tend to trigger feelings of jealousy in you?
- What types of behavior from your partner tend to trigger feelings of envy in you?

HYPOTHETICAL SCENARIOS

1. You and your partner are both interested in the same person but that person is only interested in you. How do you feel? What do you do?

_____

_____

_____

_____

_____

_____

_____

_____

_____

_____

_____

_____

_____

_____

_____

_____

_____

_____

_____

_____

_____

_____

2. Imagine the same scenario only this time the person is only interested in your partner and not you. How do you feel? What do you do?

_____

_____

_____

_____

_____

_____

_____

_____

_____

_____

_____

_____

_____

_____

_____

_____

_____

_____

_____

_____

_____

_____

3. Imagine you are the person that is interested in a relationship with one partner and not the other. How do you feel? What do you do?

-5-
What Are My Limits?

CONCEPT:

A common misconception about poly relationships is that "anything goes". It is a wonderful fantasy. The reality is, however, that everyone has core values, needs, and fears and these combine to create personal boundaries or limits. These limits are activities or behaviors that you find unacceptable because they cause damage either to you or to your relationships. Just like every other concept covered in this book, limits are unique to each individual and often evolve over time or change based on special circumstances.

It is extremely important for everyone in a poly relationship to know both their own limits and their partners' limits. Since this book is about you, this chapter will focus on identifying just your limits. I encourage you, however, to include any notes about your partners' limits that you feel will be helpful for you to reference later.

As with your needs, your limits will probably be different for each of your partners, so I have left extra space for you to include those differences in your answers. However, the format for this chapter is a bit different from the previous chapters. Instead of interspersing "Food for Thought" with the questions, I thought it would be more helpful to separate them and give you the opportunity to use my opinions to explore your own thoughts on limits in general before you began to answer any questions about your specific limits.

> ### Food for Thought
> It is natural to make sacrifices for people you love, and there is nothing wrong with a willingness to see your partner be happy even though it may cause you some emotional pain in the process. There is a big difference, however, between emotional hurt and emotional harm. It is not healthy for you or your relationships if you do not set boundaries that protect you from emotional harm.

Comments:

Every one of your limits should be given the same respect and consideration no matter how trivial they may appear. Those "small" limits can often be the remnants of sensitive areas that you have not been able to completely eliminate. For example, you might set a limit that you are the only one who is allowed to adjust the settings on the passenger seat of the car. Perhaps after years of therapy you may be able to understand why this is such a sensitive issue for you, and you might be able to relinquish partial control of the settings to another person. In my opinion, it is just so much simpler for your partner(s) to respect that limit and leave the settings alone. Also, it will reinforce your trust in your partner(s) when you see them demonstrate their willingness to put your long-term needs ahead of their temporary inconvenience.

Comments:

It is a good idea to examine your limits periodically. How do you feel about each one? Why do you have it? Have your feelings changed about it and, if so, why? Do you still need to keep the limit in place and, if not, why? It is more important to be clear about why you can let go of a limit than why you need to keep it. If you are only letting go of the limit to avoid conflict with your partner(s)' then you will simply be delaying rather than eliminating the conflict.

Comments:

It is a basic law of physics that every action causes an equal and opposite reaction. This law also applies to poly relationships. The harder you push against your partners' limits, the harder they will push to keep them in place.

Comments:

> Try not to take your partners' limits personally or view them as a lack of trust. Everyone has different personal boundaries and often these boundaries are placed and shaped by personal core values rather than past injuries. No matter why the boundary or limit exists, the most important thing to do is respect its existence.

Comments:

Giving trust requires accepting vulnerability.

Comments:

Remember, it is just as unhealthy to have a long list of limits as it is to have none. If you are uncomfortable with the limitations you are placing on your partners, try to focus on building trust – both with your partners and with yourself - so that you can eliminate those limits that are a reflection of your fears. A healthy goal to set for yourself is to control and respect your fears rather than be controlled by them.

Comments:

> I have found that my ability to trust someone else is directly related to my self-confidence. When I am feeling strong and powerful, I eagerly embrace opportunities to be vulnerable and trusting. When I doubt myself, I start doubting those around me.

Comments:

While it is admirable to try and stretch your limits as a demonstration of trust and support for your partners, be careful not to go farther or faster than you are ready to go. Try to be as honest and realistic with yourself as you possibly can. Some limits will be permanent, but others can be eliminated as the trust you have in your partners gives you the courage to tackle them and explore what lies on the other side.

Comments:

Just as you are the only one who can determine how you feel, what you want and what you need, you are also the only one who can determine what your limits will be. It is not necessary for your partners to agree that your limits are rational and logical because some of them might not be. It is important, however, that your partners understand that your goal is not to hurt them with unreasonable limits but to protect yourself and your relationships by communicating to your partners what behavior you feel is unacceptable from them.

Comments:

QUESTIONS

- Describe your limits regarding your partners' displays of affection with other people:
- Describe your limits regarding your partners' time spent with other partners:
- What are your limits regarding the types of relationships your partners' have with others?
- What limits do you have regarding your partners' activities with others?
- Describe your limits regarding commitments made by your partners' to other people:
- What are your limits regarding your personal privacy?
- Describe your limits regarding information others are given about your relationships:
- Describe your limits regarding safer sex practices:
- Describe any other limits you have that have not been addressed by the previous questions:

HYPOTHETICAL SCENARIOS

1. Your partner has stepped over one of your limits due to miscommunication. How do you feel? What do you do?

2. Your partner is very upset and believes that you overstepped a limit. You misunderstood when the limit was originally presented to you so you were unaware that what you were doing would upset your partner. How do you feel? What do you do?

3. Your partner technically does not violate a specific limit you set, but you feel the spirit of the limit was ignored. How do you feel? What do you do?

4. Your partner feels that you are not staying within the limits you agreed to accept, but you don't agree. How do you feel? What do you do?

5. One of your partners feels very frustrated by the limits set on your relationship by another one of your partners. How do you feel? What do you do?

6. You are frustrated by the limits set on your relationship by one of your partner's other partners. How do you feel? What do you do?

-6-
Family Dynamics

CONCEPT:

One of the most common poly fantasies/stereotypes is the idea of having "one big happy family". (OK, well, the "I want a harem" fantasy is probably the most common but "happy family" is definitely a close second.) By using the words "fantasies" and "stereotypes", I do not mean to imply that this kind of structure can't work or can't be a healthy way to structure your poly relationships. It can happen, I've seen it work, but it's very rare that it works. I also know some people in those types of structures well enough to be given a glimpse of what happens behind the scenes. So I know that what appears to be a smooth, seamless harmony is actually the result of careful coordination and the harmony can often get out of tune. The ones that I have seen work best are the ones who can pick up the slack when one member is having trouble keeping the tune and who can adjust the music to a less complicated arrangement when it becomes apparent that it is too difficult for most of the family to follow.

I want to make it clear that when I refer to "poly families", I am referring to any group of people who identify themselves as a "poly family". Just as every poly relationship is different, every poly family structure is different. I have known poly families who have intimate sexual relationships with everyone within the family as well as poly families where there are no sexual relationships within the family. Most poly families fall somewhere between these two extremes, but the bonds of family are just as strong no matter what structure holds them. Poly family bonds exist by choice. It is the strength of the commitment to the relationships that provides the "glue" for the bonds, and the structure of the family provides the pathways for those bonds to be utilized in a way that best suits the family and the individuals within the family.

Even though it is a great deal of work, being a member of a poly family does have great benefits and can be especially valuable for people who do not have the support of their biological family. Every person has a unique perspective on life, a set of skills, and physical resources. One benefit of being part of a poly family is that you can draw upon some or all of those resources when needed. Whether the goal is for the betterment of the community or specifically for the benefit of the family, the group as a whole can accomplish far more by working together than any of the individuals could accomplish working separately.

On the other hand, being a member of a poly family is certainly not an ideal situation for everyone, whether they identify as polyamorous or not. If you have a strong need for privacy and personal independence, then a poly family dynamic is probably not for you.

Hopefully, your answers to the questions in the previous chapters have enabled you to determine whether or not you are suited to a poly family dynamic. The rest of this chapter assumes that you have decided that you are suited to a poly family structure, so there are no questions to answer or hypothetical scenarios to ponder. What follows are some insights and guidance for those who have chosen to be in a poly family. I have still left space for you to write your own comments on each bit of "Food for Thought".

> **Food for Thought**
> If you are experiencing some dysfunction in your poly family, take a moment and think about your own childhood. Was the same dysfunctional behavior present in your biological family? Was the dysfunction ever corrected? How much of your behavior do you think could be contributing to the current problems? Are you simply repeating familiar childhood patterns?

Comments:

> Sometimes a "peer pressure" develops within poly families for each person to be willing and able to give whatever it takes to "feed" the other relationships. The needs of each individual should be given the same respect as the needs of the family and the relationships within the family. When conflicting needs arise, discuss them with the goal of finding a way to reaffirm the importance of the family's commitment to the individual and the individual's commitment to the family. The commitments go both ways and should be upheld both ways.

Comments:

_____

_____

_____

_____

_____

_____

_____

_____

_____

_____

_____

_____

_____

_____

_____

_____

Among the many reasons it is critical for people in poly relationships to communicate is simple logistics. This is especially true with poly families because it is important that plans be communicated so everyone feels included. Even if your structure allows individuals to choose whether or not to participate in family events and it is not something some members would normally choose to do - invite them anyway. People join poly families for a sense of inclusion so it is important to make sure that they feel welcome and included.

Comments:

In poly families, each person generally ends up with a specific role in the family. Some are assigned but most just develop (i.e., peacemaker, comic relief, organizer, messenger, etc.). All relationships require a certain amount of work to keep them going and that work is significantly greater in a poly family dynamic. It is extremely important that each individual family member is aware of what the other members are doing for the family so that one person does not become overwhelmed. It is equally important to speak up and ask for help from the rest of the family when you are feeling overburdened.

Comments:

_____

_____

_____

_____

_____

_____

_____

_____

_____

_____

_____

_____

_____

_____

_____

_____

_____

Part of the work of being in a poly family is not just "feeding" your relationship with the family as a whole but also maintaining your relationship with each individual within the family. Since each person is different, your individual relationships within the family will be unique with each person.

However, even if you have the same level of commitment to each person, schedules and logistics will often create situations where you spend more time interacting with some members of the family than with others. When this happens, it is very easy to fall into the trap of talking *through* each other rather than talking *to* each other. When messages and news start getting passed through others on a regular basis, the potential for miscommunication and false assumptions increases dramatically. If there is something you want someone in the family to know, make sure to say it directly to that individual. This will serve a double purpose of diminishing the potential for miscommunication and reaffirming the importance of your individual relationships.

Comments:

When you are having difficulties with someone in your poly family, other people in the family are valuable sources of advice and counsel on how to resolve the problem. Be very cautious, however, in how you approach other people for this advice. First of all, if you have a problem with someone, it is important to try to resolve the problem with that person first before you involve anyone else. Oftentimes the problem is a simple miscommunication that can be resolved without involving anyone else in the family. If you are still unable to resolve the problem and you wish to talk to other family members about it, make sure that you are seeking advice to resolve the problem and not simply looking for allies to take your side in a disagreement. Finally, focus on getting advice about what *you* should do to alleviate the difficulty rather than just complaining about what you think the other person is doing wrong.

Comments:

Even though you have individual relationships with each member of your poly family, those relationships do not exist in a vacuum and they impact every other member of the family. In fact, everything in your life has the potential to impact every member of the family so it is very important that you understand the responsibility that comes with that connection. Also, membership in a family goes both ways - you claim connection to them and they claim connection to you. This means that your actions not only impact your family, but they are also a reflection on your family. As a member of a poly family, you are no longer acting as a sole individual; you are responsible to the family and for the family.

Comments:

_____

_____

_____

_____

_____

_____

_____

_____

_____

_____

_____

_____

_____

_____

_____

-7-
Negotiation

CONCEPT:

The previous chapters have been designed to prepare you for the next step in the process of developing a poly relationship – negotiation. As with everything else about poly relationships, the negotiation process will be unique to each individual and each relationship. There is no "right" way to successfully negotiate a poly relationship – although there are many "wrong" ways. Since I have successfully negotiated several poly relationships by vastly different methods, I think that giving an account of those negotiations will give you a clear understanding of just how varied your options for negotiation can be and why one method may be preferable over another based on circumstances.

When I negotiated my first poly relationship, my primary partner and I had not had any poly relationships that we would consider successful. We still believed that it *could* be done; we just weren't entirely sure *how* to make it work for us. My potential partner and his wife had a bit more experience and knowledge than we did, but very little personal experience with an on-going, long-term poly relationship – which is what we were seeking. I went into the negotiation process knowing that at the very least I wanted to have a close friendship with both my potential partner and his wife and anything else beyond that I would consider a "bonus".

Since the relationship dynamic I shared with my primary partner at the time was a Master/slave relationship, I had agreed that it was completely up to him as my Master whether or not I would enter into a poly relationship and the boundaries of that relationship. I had met my potential partner and his wife, I knew that I was definitely interested in him, I had a pretty good indication that the interest was mutual, so I talked to my partner and let him know about my interest. My partner had not yet met my potential partner and his wife so that was the first step in the process. When I told my partner about my interest in a poly relationship, I also told him that I was fairly certain that at the very least we would want to be good friends with the couple. Logistics were a little complicated because we lived 5 hours away from them, but we often traveled near where they lived so we arranged to spend some time with them on one of our trips.

That meeting went well and a few days later, my partner called my potential partner to let him know of my interest, and that he had given me permission to explore the possibility. My potential partner told my partner that he needed to discuss it with his wife before he could negotiate anything with my partner. After they talked, he called my partner and let him know that she had given her approval to further the discussions.

It was very important for me that my potential partner's wife be comfortable with any arrangements we made. As I said, I liked them both and wanted to make sure I didn't do anything that could ruin a potentially great friendship. So, before discussions went any further, I arranged to come up and spend the evening with the two of them so that she could get to know me better. Even though my potential partner was present, 90% of the conversation was between me and his wife. We didn't get into specific details, we simply talked about our general philosophies about poly relationships and how we envisioned those relationships would be structured.

After my talk with his wife, everyone felt comfortable enough to begin discussing the specifics of the relationship. This time they came to visit us for the weekend, and during that time my partner and my potential partner negotiated the boundaries of the poly relationship he and I would have. After that discussion, my partner gave his final approval to the relationship, and the way was clear for me and my potential partner to discuss what we wanted from each other within the boundaries set by our primary partners.

That process took three months, but he and I instinctively knew that we had the potential for something really great and we were willing to take it slow and build the right foundation to make the relationship last. It was a little awkward when he and I finally began to discuss the specifics with each other, because we had talked about it with everyone else, but had never actually said "I want you" to each other. I joke that it was kind of like being in high school – a "my friend told your friend to tell you that I might like you" kind of feeling. It was far more formal than most poly negotiations are conducted, but the caution and formality were necessary for everyone to feel comfortable with the relationship.

Since my primary partner was my Master, we had agreed that he would have much more freedom in choosing his partners and negotiating the relationships. Even so, he valued my opinion and included me in the process when he initiated new relationships. Those negotiations were generally along the lines of the conversations I had with my additional partner's wife – general philosophies and relationship structures. I had set boundaries and limits for his relationships, but those negotiations took place between me and my primary partner just as my additional partner and his wife had discussed her limits and boundaries for his relationships.

In contrast to those styles of negotiation, around the time I started writing this book, I decided that it would be a good idea for me to be open to the idea of a new relationship, and both of my partners were in favor of this idea. Even though I was still an owned slave (although by this time my primary partner had given ownership of me to my additional partner), I was given complete freedom to choose and negotiate any new relationship. My additional partner simply reserved the right to "veto" the relationship if it proved to be unhealthy for me at any time.

Oddly enough, the very night I received the permission to pursue a new relationship, I found my new partner through an online personal ad. Since he was single, our negotiation process was conducted just between the two of us. That "process" simply consisted of conversations about what we each had to offer the other in a relationship and we each wanted out of a relationship. The other reason our negotiations were never formal was that my life situation underwent some dramatic changes shortly after we began our relationship, so I wasn't in a position to set a definite foundation for the new relationship until the rest of my life was more settled. I want to emphasize, however, that just because we never labeled our conversations as negotiations, that is, indeed, what occurred. In fact, virtually every question covered in the first chapters of this book was addressed within the first two weeks of meeting each other.

All of the negotiation methods I have described above were the "right" ones for the situation and people involved. The goal was to set a solid foundation and framework for the new relationships. The type of relationship desired and how it would be integrated into existing relationships dictated what process would accomplish that goal.

> ### Food for Thought
>
> Since there are many different ways to negotiate poly relationships, you may find that the first item you end up negotiating is the negotiation process itself if the parties involved have needs to be met by the process. One of the most common pieces of advice given by poly practitioners applies here – let the person who is least comfortable with the process or relationship set the pace.

Comments:

Remember this book is made of paper, not stone. You are probably not using blood to write in it (if you are – cool!). The point is that nothing has to be permanent. Figure out what will work for now but leave room for change in the future.

Comments:

_____

_____

_____

_____

_____

_____

_____

_____

_____

_____

_____

_____

_____

_____

_____

_____

_____

_____

_____

_____

Each relationship you add to your life has the potential to dramatically increase your happiness. However, it also has the potential to destroy your other relationships. Tread slowly and softly.

Comments:

> Building relationships is like building houses. If you do not take the time to lay the proper foundation, the relationship will never be stable no matter how much time and effort you put into patching and fixing the problems.

Comments:

A key point to remember in negotiating poly relationships is that one person's joy may be another person's burden. We all have many things to offer our poly partners; negotiation enables us to identify those things that are mutually satisfying rather than draining. To use the houseplant example again, I once accepted a houseplant as a housewarming gift from someone who did not know me very well. She loved plants and found great joy in caring for them. She also has one of the most open and giving hearts I've known, and I wanted to honor those qualities I admired so much in her by accepting her gift. In spite of my limitations, I managed to keep that plant alive for over 4 years and passed it to someone else when I had to move and couldn't take it with me. I kept the plant alive to honor the woman who gave it to me, but I did not find any joy in caring for the plant. Instead of being a symbol of life and love, it became a burden and a source of guilt for me when my lack of care would become obvious.

Comments:

> Negotiation can be viewed as deliberately setting realistic expectations rather than making unrealistic assumptions.

Comments:

_____

_____

_____

_____

_____

_____

_____

_____

_____

_____

_____

_____

_____

_____

_____

_____

_____

_____

_____

_____

_____

Negotiation within a poly relationship should be approached in a completely different manner than negotiation within a business relationship. Successful business negotiators have the goal of getting the most from the other party while giving the least to the other party. In business, it is a competitive spirit that succeeds. Successful poly relationship negotiators have the goal of making sure everyone's needs are met while preserving as many partners' wants as possible. In poly, it is a cooperative spirit that succeeds.

Comments:

-8-
Preventive Medicine

CONCEPT

So ... you have successfully negotiated your new poly relationship and are ready to begin living "happily ever after". Unfortunately, preparing for the trip and actually being on the journey are two very different things. No matter how thoroughly you negotiated your relationship, there will always be something unexpected that comes along – either something that was unanticipated or something that was considered but not thought to be an issue. I have titled this chapter "Preventive Medicine" because the thoughts that follow are designed to help you anticipate issues so that you can address them before they become problems. Continual doses of "preventive medicine" will also help keep your relationships healthy enough to get through the times when the potential issues become real problems.

> Food for Thought
> Instead of thinking about a relationship or a person as "yours", try thinking of it as a cherished object on loan to you. The loan may be for a short time or a lifetime. Whatever the case, you will want to show your gratitude by returning it undamaged and perhaps in better condition than when you received it.

Comments:
_____
_____
_____
_____
_____
_____
_____
_____
_____
_____

> As the saying goes, good things come to those who wait. I have found that by exercising a little patience, I can get far more than I would if I had given in to the impulse for instant gratification.

Comments:

_____

_____

_____

_____

_____

_____

_____

_____

_____

_____

_____

_____

_____

_____

_____

_____

_____

_____

_____

_____

_____

> Trust is a gift that is meant to be shared. It should not be given lightly, nor should it be accepted without an understanding of the responsibilities of safeguarding the gift from harm.

Comments:

> When you find yourself staring at the walls of the limits set by your partner(s), try turning around to see all of the wonderful things that exist within those boundaries.

Comments:

_____

_____

_____

_____

_____

_____

_____

_____

_____

_____

_____

_____

_____

_____

_____

_____

_____

_____

_____

_____

_____

_____

> Be very protective of your personal ethics. What is right for someone else may not be "right" for you. In the end, you are the one who has to face yourself in the mirror and you are the only one who can determine what will allow you to love what you see in that mirror.

Comments:

> Just because something has not been expressed as a limit by your partner(s), do not assume that it is fine to do it. If you haven't discussed something or feel a "twist" in your stomach regarding something you've already discussed, follow your gut instincts. If you are feeling even a twinge of doubt, stop and wait until you can discuss things with your partner(s). Not only can this help you avoid problems, it will build your partner(s)' trust in you.

Comments:

> Keep in mind that when you first start your new relationship, the relationship and changes are new to your other partner(s) as well. While a certain amount of trust already exists or the relationships would not exist, that trust is new and needs a great deal of care and feeding.

Comments:

_____

_____

_____

_____

_____

_____

_____

_____

_____

_____

_____

_____

_____

_____

_____

_____

_____

_____

_____

_____

_____

There is a saying that it is easier to get forgiveness than permission. This might be true, but it is also true that too much instant gratification could result in an instant ending to your relationships.

Comments:

As you learn and grow as a person, your needs and wants will change. It is important to communicate these changes and renegotiate the framework of your relationship to reflect your new needs. The renegotiation process can be stressful, but the stress will be minimized if you view it as a result of success in personal awareness rather than a failure by either party to anticipate the changes you are destined to undergo.

Comments:

_____

_____

_____

_____

_____

_____

_____

_____

_____

_____

_____

_____

_____

_____

_____

_____

_____

_____

_____

_____

Communicating with your partner(s) about problems is essential for the long-term success of your relationships. However, there is a difference between communicating to resolve an on-going problem and complaining about a momentary discomfort. A good rule of thumb to follow is to ask yourself, "Will this bother me tomorrow?" If the answer is no, then you should let it drop. If the answer is yes, then you have an obligation to discuss the situation with your partner(s) rather than harbor a resentment that will create a barrier to the trust you have built together.

Comments:

> Keep in mind that it is fairly easy to be "perfect" for a weekend but impossible to do so on a daily basis. It is unfair to hold your live-in partner(s) to the same standards that are set by the partner(s) you see on an occasional basis.

Comments:

_____

_____

_____

_____

_____

_____

_____

_____

_____

_____

_____

_____

_____

_____

_____

_____

_____

_____

_____

_____

Most of us did not grow up in poly households so we have very limited exposure to healthy, successful poly relationships. Seeking out connections with other poly people is an excellent way to build a "resource bank" to draw upon for advice and ideas on how to improve your relationships. However, participation in poly support groups shouldn't be limited to people who are seeking help. You could be an asset in someone else's resource bank if your poly relationships are working well for you and you make the time to share your experience with others who are struggling.

Comments:

Poly relationships are like intricate dances. It requires practice and coordination among all participants to get the "steps and rhythms" right. In the meantime, someone is bound to stub their toes or step on someone's foot by mistake. Be patient with each other and try to keep in mind that the mistakes are unintentional when this happens.

Comments:

I do not use "absolute" words lightly but this is one case I will make an exception. *Never* encourage or allow your partner(s) to compete for your affection, because nothing will destroy healthy poly relationships faster than competition among the participants. This "no competition" rule applies to you as well; do not compare your partner(s) to each other. If you find yourself mentally comparing them, stop immediately because your thoughts will soon translate into actions that will spell disaster.

Comments:

-9-
Problem Solving

CONCEPT

People make mistakes. Since poly relationships involve many people, the potential for mistakes and problems increases dramatically with each new relationship added to the mixture. It is very important that everyone goes into the relationship knowing that problems are bound to occur and be committed to working together to find solutions to the problems when that happens.

The first step in resolving problems is communication. The parties involved need to know that a problem exists in order for them to correct it. The focus of the communication should be the cause of the problem rather than the symptoms. The symptoms are *what* happened; the cause is *why* it happened. Without addressing the cause, the problem will continue to occur.

Once you have figured out what is causing the problem, the next step is to figure out what needs to be done to eliminate the cause. Sometimes the answer is as simple as having a central communication board in the house, but sometimes the only way to solve the problem is to create a major change in how the relationships are structured. I will emphasize again the importance of working *together* in this phase. Working together helps strengthen trust in relationships and that trust has probably been broken or weakened as a result of the problem so it will need that demonstration of commitment to stay strong. If one person begins to feel that it is a Them vs. Me situation, that person is going to become defensive and lose even more trust in the relationship. If everyone accepts responsibility for the existence of the problem, then it will be easier to avoid the trap of placing blame and this also acknowledges that everyone involved will be feeling some amount of hurt and anger over the situation.

Unfortunately, there are times when problems can't be resolved, or the only solution to the problem requires something that is unacceptable to one or more of the people involved. It is also an inescapable fact of life that everything and everyone changes, and sometimes those changes mean that one or more people simply lose interest in the relationship. In both of those cases, the solution to the problem becomes ending one or more of the relationships. This should be viewed as a last resort "solution", but if you view it as a solution rather than as a failure, it will make the transition much easier for everyone. Everyone should be committed to working together to find the solution, and they should carry that commitment into ending the poly relationship(s) in a way that minimizes the pain and preserves as much trust in each other as possible.

No matter what solution is found to the problem, enacting the change required by the solution will involve some level of difficulty for everyone involved. Just as it was important to be patient with each other at the beginning of the relationship, it is important to maintain that patience while the changes are occurring. Part of exercising that patience may be giving each other space to grieve. Regardless of whether the change involves a simple behavior modification or what benefits the change will bring, any change involves a loss of some kind, and each person may need to grieve that loss as part of the healing process for the relationship(s).

The information found in this "concept" and the "food for thought" that follows is merely a tip of the iceberg. An entire book could easily be devoted to this subject alone. Although this chapter doesn't provide all of the answers, it is my hope that it has at least given you some solid guidance in your search for those answers. I am not a trained therapist or counselor. The advice in this chapter represents my own opinions based on lessons learned from personal experience and learning from the experience of others. Depending on the severity of the problems, it may be wise to seek help from a counselor to facilitate the process of communication and resolution. Finally, if at any time you believe the relationship has become physically or emotionally abusive, seek immediate help from appropriate authorities and/or qualified professionals

---

Food for Thought
No one wants to make mistakes. However, mistakes can be turned into successes if you take the time to analyze why the mistake occurred and take steps to insure that it does not happen in the future. Mistakes are inevitable, but foresight and hindsight should be used to reduce their frequency.

Comments:

QUESTIONS

- ❧ The most important question you can ever ask yourself when you are experiencing difficulties is "why". Why do I feel this way? Why am I acting this way? Why did I say that?
- ❧ The second most important question you can ever ask yourself when faced with difficulties is "what". What am I afraid of? What do I want? What do I need? What actions can I take to help the situation?
- ❧ No one is perfect. It is how a person handles their own imperfections and mistakes that determines whether or not he/she is trustworthy. How do you handle yours?
- ❧ The spirit speaks with a quiet voice. When you are having trouble finding answers to your difficulties, your spirit may have the answers you seek if you can be still and listen to what it is telling you. What is Spirit saying to you now?

Afterword

When I finished the first draft of this book, I asked a couple of people to read it and give me their opinions. One comment was unanimous – I should not end the book with the Problem Solving chapter. I needed to add something more so the book would end on a positive note. This is truly a poly "workbook" - it requires work to complete and it emphasizes the amount of work required to successfully manage healthy poly relationships. If it is that difficult, why bother?

As I said in the beginning of this book, I see poly relationships (and life) as a journey. Climbing Mount Everest requires a great deal of preparation, work, significant risk, and a bit of good luck. Quite frankly, I see it as a recipe for misery and disaster. However, for the people who dream of being one of the few to "stand on the top of the world", the thrill of success far outweighs the hardships encountered along the way. In fact, the thrill of success is made even sweeter by the self-satisfaction gained from meeting and overcoming those challenges. Poly relationships are not for everyone, but for some of us the rewards to be found are well worth risking the hazards of the journey.

For me, I am living out my dreams as I share my life with other people through my poly relationships. It hasn't always been roses and chocolate. There have been times when I felt I would not recover from the pain caused by a poly relationship going astray. I have experienced the feelings of abandonment, betrayal, and rejection in ways and levels of intensity I never imagined possible. However, as a result of surviving those experiences, my self-confidence and sense of self-worth increased dramatically.

In the past, I avoided emotional vulnerability and saw it as an unhealthy behavior that I needed to eliminate in order to be happy. Through my poly relationships, I have learned that emotional vulnerability is an important ingredient in a healthy relationship. I cannot grow as a person, I cannot have the level of intimacy I want in my relationships, and I cannot be open to new relationships (poly or otherwise) if I am not willing to be emotionally vulnerable. I found happiness when I stopped trying to eliminate my emotional vulnerability and learned to embrace it instead.

Looking back, I can see that my lack of self-confidence caused me to avoid situations where I would be emotionally vulnerable. I only equated vulnerability with weakness, victimization and pain. Ironically, it was through the intense pain that came when things went wrong in my poly relationships that I eventually learned that allowing emotional vulnerability is actually a demonstration of strength, not weakness. I was vulnerable, I got hurt, I survived, and I was willing to stay vulnerable so that the relationship could continue. It took a great deal of strength and self-confidence to keep going in spite of the pain.

Just because I chose to continue a relationship that had caused me emotional pain did not mean I allowed myself to be a victim. I was no different than the mountain climber on Everest who slips off the cliff face and breaks an arm. I could give up and go home, or I could figure out a way to keep going in spite of the added difficulty. I believed in myself and my relationships, so I kept going. The short-term pain was worth the long-term benefits. If I had let the pain rule my decisions, then I would have been a victim.

However, as I mentioned in the beginning of this book, I have ended a poly relationship, so I have not always chosen to continue. In that particular case, we had been to the "top of the mountain" together and shared the joy and thrill of accomplishing our common goals. Unfortunately, people change, and sometimes that means their goals and dreams change, too. In this case, in order for both of us to achieve success, we had to accept the short-term pain of giving up the comfort and stability of an established partnership. Once again, it was personal strength and self-confidence that allowed me to embrace vulnerability and pursue my dreams.

As strong and capable as I believe myself to be, I still would not have had the emotional, physical and spiritual resources to survive the past several years on my own. My life has been completely turned upside down and shaken. With the help of my poly relationships and poly family, I have not merely survived but I have found new happiness and joy. Knowing that I could draw upon the strength and resources of my poly family enabled me to view each change as an opportunity for growth. I do not feel defeated; I feel that I accomplished my goals on one path, but there is more for me to accomplish and I must change direction in order to find success. Regardless of where that path takes me, I won't be making the journey on my own; others will be there with me to give me strength, courage, and assistance when I need them.

As I move into the next stages of my journey, I will admit that I have moments of fear and self-doubt. I am fully aware of the risks I am taking and the consequences of making a wrong step. However, I know that no matter what lies ahead, as long as I keep going, I am living out my dreams. I have healthy poly relationships and I belong to a wonderful poly family. I love and I am loved. For me, there is no greater thrill or success to be found in life.

About The Author

Christina "slavette" Parker has balanced multiple relationships and several alternative lifestyles since 1996. Best known for her work in the leather and BDSM communities, she was a collared slave from 1996-2009. With her first Master, Christina was honored to receive the Pantheon of Leather Awards for Couple of the Year (2001) and Small Event of the Year for Together in Leather 2004 as well as hold the title of International slave 2002.

As part of her commitment to community service and activism, Christina has served as Fundraising Director for the National Coalition for Sexual Freedom (NCSF), served on the Board of Directors for CUFF, SSCN and Gnosis, and has been a founding member of four BDSM educational/support/social groups.

Christina has given over 200 workshops across the U.S. and in Canada. She was an instructor for Apex Academy/Butchman's Experience in Phoenix, AZ and serves as a guest instructor for Master Taino's Training Academy as needed. While she speaks on a variety of topics, her primary educational focus is on polyamorous relationships, M/s relationships, service, sacred sexuality, and spirituality. Christina is the author of *Where I am Led: A Service Exploration Workbook* and a columnist for Sexis Magazine.

CPSIA information can be obtained
at www.ICGtesting.com
Printed in the USA
BVHW060718040821
613437BV00006B/548